ANISHINAABE

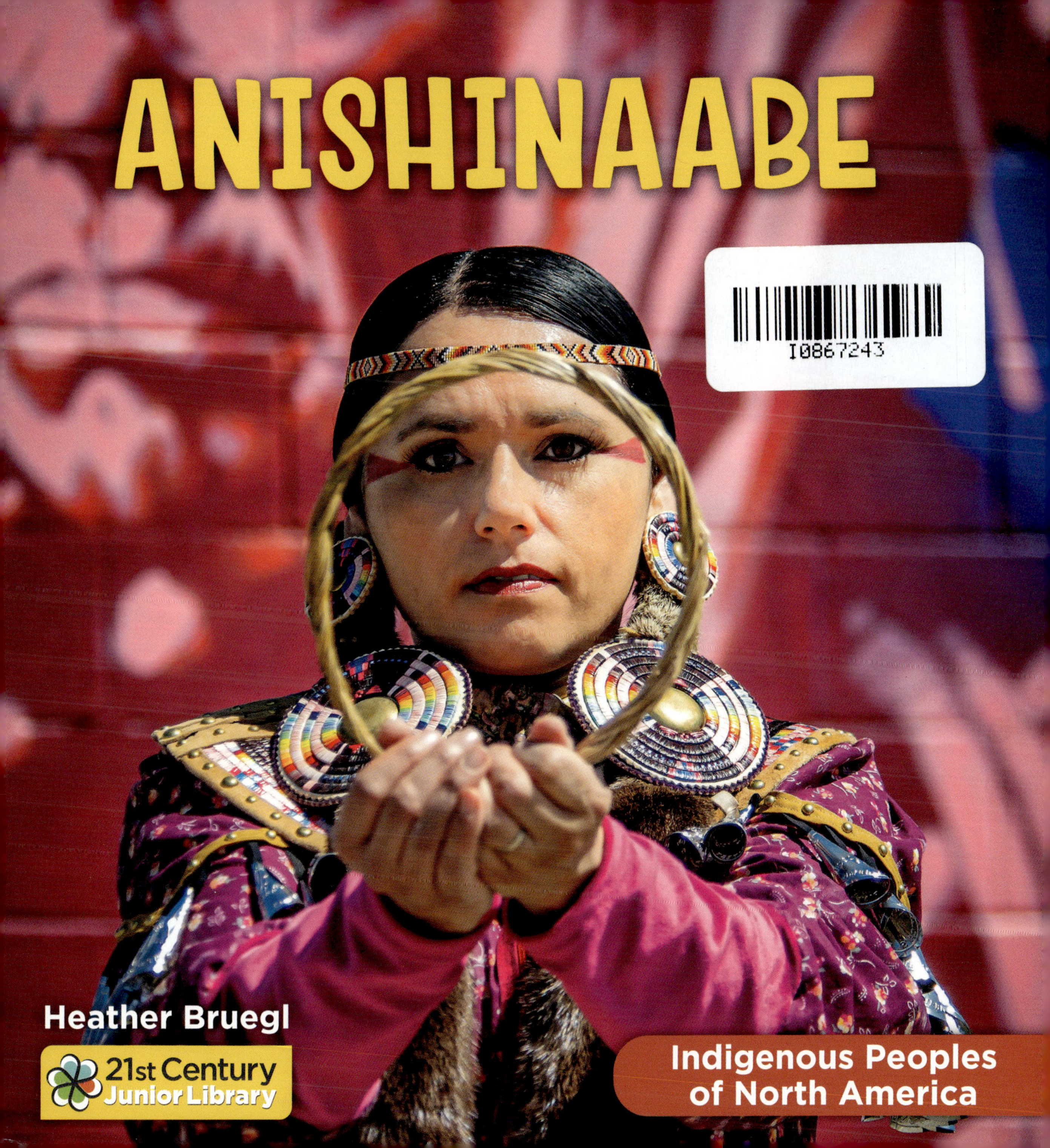

Heather Bruegl

21st Century Junior Library

Indigenous Peoples of North America

Published in the United States of America by:

Cherry Lake Press
2395 South Huron Parkway, Suite 200, Ann Arbor, Michigan 48104
www.cherrylakepress.com

Reading Adviser: Beth Walker Gambro, MS, Ed., Reading Consultant, Yorkville, IL
Content Advisers: Grey Shea, Cultural Language Educator, Bay Mills Indian Community, Ogimaag-Gamig Governmental Center; Matthew Fletcher, JD, Harry Burns Hutchins Collegiate Professor of Law at Michigan Law, writing and teaching on Anishinaabe legal and political philosophy, among many other topics

Photo Credits: © Michelle Reed, Photograph by Chad Coppess, cover and title page; © ZUMA Press Inc/Alamy Stock Photo, 5; © ASSOCIATED PRESS, 6; © 2011 Minnesota Public Radio®, Used with permission, 9; © 2020 Minnesota Public Radio®, Used with permission, 11; NPS Photos/Jacob W. Frank, 13; © Mike Worley Photos/Shutterstock, 14; © Nottawaseppi Huron Band of the Potawatomi via NHBP.PassGallery, 16, 21; © 2019 Minnesota Public Radio®, Used with permission, 19

Cherry Lake Press is an imprint of Cherry Lake Publishing Group.

Library of Congress Cataloging-in-Publication Data

Names: Bruegl, Heather, author.
Title: Anishinaabe / written by: Heather Bruegl.
Description: Ann Arbor, MI : Cherry Lake Publishing, [2025] | Series: Indigenous peoples of North America | Includes bibliographical references and index. | Audience: Grades 2-3 | Summary: "The Anishinaabe peoples share language, culture, and history that connect them in many ways. In this introduction to the Council of Three Fires, readers learn about the Ojibwa, Potawatomi, and Odawa peoples, land, history, and accomplishments. Written by Indigenous author and public historian, Heather Bruegl, a citizen of the Oneida Nation and first-line descendent Strockbridge-Munsee, this series provides a simple and authentic introduction to the unique cultures and peoples that have made this continent home for thousands of years, and are still here today"– Provided by publisher.
Identifiers: LCCN 2024036514 | ISBN 9781668956243 (hardcover) | ISBN 9781668957097 (paperback) | ISBN 9781668957967 (ebook) | ISBN 9781668958834 (pdf)
Subjects: LCSH: Ojibwa Indians–Juvenile literature.
Classification: LCC E99.C6 B86 2025 | DDC 977.004/97333–dc23/eng/20240925
LC record available at https://lccn.loc.gov/2024036514

Cherry Lake Publishing would like to acknowledge the work of the Partnership for 21st Century Learning, a network of Battelle for Kids. Please visit Battelle for Kids online for more information.

Printed in the United States of America

Note from publisher: Websites change regularly, and their future contents are outside of our control.
Supervise children when conducting any recommended online searches for extended learning opportunities.

About the Cover: Michelle Reed is an enrolled member of the Lac du Flambeau Band of Ojibwe. She lives in the Upper Peninsula of Michigan with her husband and their two children. She dances jingle, hoop, traditional, and fancy shawl. She is the manager and co-founder of the Woodland Sky Native American Dance Company as well as lead female dancer for the #1 selling Native American recording group Brulé. She has developed N8V Dance Fitness and is a clothing and accessories designer, doing custom sewing and beadwork for many champion dancers as well as a full purse line, MReed Designs Purse Co. Her latest project is the Indigenous Girl Doll Collection.

CONTENTS

WHO WE ARE

The word *Anishinaabe* has several meanings. It can mean "original man" or "good human." The Anishinaabe are not one group. They are a large group of peoples connected by a common language. They are connected by similar traditions and culture, too.

Different tribal nations make up the Anishinaabe. Each nation has its own name and meaning. Each has its own traditions and history. The Ojibwe are

An Ojibwe youth learns traditional wild rice farming in Minnesota.

the largest Anishinaabe group. They are sometimes called the Chippewa. The Ojibwe are one of three members of the Council of Three Fires. That is a **confederation** between the Ojibwe, Odawa (Ottawa), and Bodewadmi (Potawatomi) peoples. The Anishinaabe also includes other **Algonquin**-speaking peoples. Anishinaabemowin is the Anishinaabe language.

Lac La Croix First Nation speaker Gordon Jourdain shares traditional Ojibwe tales.

Make a Guess!

Can you guess which Anishinaabe word means "good" in the text below? If you guessed *mino*, you were right!

In Anishinaabe culture, all living things are sacred. Life, or ***bimaadiziwin***, should have balance and harmony. People should work for *mino-bimaadiziwin*. This means a good life. A good life is one of collective well-being. It is one where people look out for each other.

OUR LIVES TODAY

Hundreds of thousands of Anishinaabe peoples live in the United States and Canada. It is one of the largest cultural groups in North America. The Ojibwe have the largest population. Many Anishinaabe people live in Michigan, Wisconsin, and Minnesota. Some also live in Oklahoma. In Canada, the Anishinaabe live mostly in parts of Ontario.

But these are not the only places they live. Anishinaabe peoples actively take part in American and Canadian life. They are teachers, lawyers, nurses,

Traditional Anishinaabe wild rice harvesting is an important connection to the land.

government leaders, business owners, farmers, and every job in between. Anishinaabe military members also serve around the globe.

Anishinaabe people play important roles in the arts, media, and history. They include Olympic ski jumper Steve Collins and actor Adam Beach. They also include boxer Mary Spencer and fastpitch softball pitcher Darren Zack.

Ask Questions!

What else do you want to know about Anishinaabe life today? How can you find answers to your questions?

Brenda Child is an Ojibwe author and scholar. Here she is with her daughter Benay.

Many Anishinaabe nations, such as the Ojibwe, still live on **ancestral** lands. Some live on **unceded territory**. Non-Indigenous people live in these places, too. There is often a struggle to protect Indigenous **sovereignty**.

For example, the Ojibwe have a **treaty** right to spearfish in Wisconsin. Spearfishing is a traditional practice. Non-Indigenous fishermen protested this right. The conflict was called the Walleye War. Walleye is a type of fish. The issue went to court. Wisconsin courts ruled that the Ojibwe's right to spearfish in the lakes of their ancestors was protected by treaty.

Protecting their Indigenous ways of life is an important issue. So is preserving the Anishinaabemowin language and Anishinaabe traditions and culture. Many tribes have language and culture departments. Two large organizations are the Ojibwe Cultural Foundation and the Wikwemikong Heritage Organization.

Look!

What can you tell about traditional spearfishing from this picture?

Many Anishinaabe peoples still make the Great Lakes region their home in both the United States and Canada.

OUR ANCESTRAL LANDS

According to **oral traditions**, the Anishinaabe first lived in the eastern United States and Canada. They moved westward to the shores of Lake Superior.

In Canada, Anishinaabe traditional lands stretch through northern Ontario and parts of Saskatchewan. They include the Ottawa Valley. In the United States, their land included northern North Dakota, Minnesota, and Michigan. It also included the lakeshores of Lakes Ontario and Lake Erie. **Forced removal** later drove many out of the Great Lakes region.

Just like many other tribal nations, the Anishinaabe people value their relationship with the land. They protect the land. They understand that caring for it is vital to Earth's survival. The land **nourishes** the body.

Wild rice grows throughout Anishinaabe land.

Before European **colonization**, the Anishinaabe fished and hunted traditional game. They ate local nuts and berries. They harvested wild rice. They tapped maple trees to make syrup and candy. They also farmed large areas of land. Women were in charge of the farms. They learned to plant crops in patterns that helped them grow. This was the **Three Sisters** method. It was how they grew corn, squash, and beans. They passed this knowledge to their children. They believed their responsibility was to protect the land for the next seven generations.

Think!

Think about what you know about nutrition. How does Anishinaabe land provide everything needed to be healthy?

CARRYING TRADITIONS FORWARD

The Anishinaabe have a vibrant culture rooted in storytelling and art. Art forms include creating baskets from birch bark and ash wood. Many baskets have traditional designs using porcupine quills. Beads were used in basket designs after the Anishinaabe made contact with Europeans. This practice of basket making is active today.

Dance is also deeply rooted in Anishinaabe culture. The Jingle Dance is popular at powwows across North

America. It began as an Ojibwe dance in 1920. An Ojibwe man had a dream about the dance. He woke up and either made a dress or had it made. The dress was decorated with many tin cones. The cones were formed by curling the tops of tin cans. The cones were then sewn into the dress. When the fabric moved, the cones jingled like bells. One story says the man's daughter was sick. She wore the dress and danced like in his dream. She then got well.

Create!

With an adult, go online and create a playlist of different jingle dances. Note what is the same and different. How do the dancers use their dresses as instruments?

The Anishinaabe use art to keep traditions alive. They also rely on teachings to guide their lives. These are the Seven Grandfather Teachings. They include love, truth, wisdom, humility, respect, courage, and honesty. The Anishinaabe still follow these values and teachings.

Drumming is still an important part of Anishinaabe life and culture today.

GLOSSARY

Algonquin (al-GAHN-kwuhn) an Indigenous language group that includes similar languages

ancestral (an-SEH-struhl) belonging to past generations of a family or cultural group

colonization (kah-luh-nuh-ZAY-shuhn) the act of settling in an area and exercising control over Indigenous peoples

confederation (kuhn-feh-duh-RAY-shuhn) a league or alliance between different groups to work toward common goals

forced removal (FORST rih-MOO-vuhl) the removal of Indigenous peoples by force to another location away from their traditional homeland

nourishes (NER-ih-shuhz) helps to grow and thrive

oral traditions (OR-uhl truh-DIH-shuhnz) verbal accounts of history, songs, and languages and how these are passed down

sovereignty (SAH-vruhn-tee) freedom from outside rule or control

Three Sisters (THREE SIH-sterz) a form of planting in Indigenous communities that refers to the planting of corn, beans, and squash

treaty (TREE-tee) a legal document similar to a contract that is signed between nations

unceded territory (uhn-SEE-ded TAIR-uh-tor-ee) land that was not given up with a sale or treaty

FIND OUT MORE

Books

Buchholtz, Julie. *Who Am I?* Ann Arbor, MI: Sleeping Bear Press, 2023.

Child, Brenda. *Bowwow Powwow*. St. Paul, MN: Minnesota Historical Society Press, 2018.

Shoulders, Michael and Debbie Shoulders. *D is for Drum: A Native American Alphabet*. Ann Arbor, MI: Sleeping Bear Press, 2006.

Sorell, Traci. *We Are Still Here! Native American Truths Everyone Should Know*. Watertown, MA: Charlesbridge, 2021.

Online

With an adult, explore more online with these suggested searches.

- "The Ojibwe People," Minnesota Historical Society
- "Museum," Ojibwe Cultural Foundation

Say Hello!

Aanii (ah-nee) is Anishinaabemowin for "Hi."

INDEX

ABOUT THE AUTHOR

Heather Bruegl, a member of the Oneida Nation of Wisconsin/Stockbridge-Munsee, is a Madonna University graduate with a Master of Arts in U.S. History. She is a public historian and decolonial educator, and her Munsee name is Kiishookunkwe, which means "Sunflower in Full Bloom." Heather frequently travels to present on Indigenous history, policy, and activism, bringing her deep knowledge and personal connection to the subject.